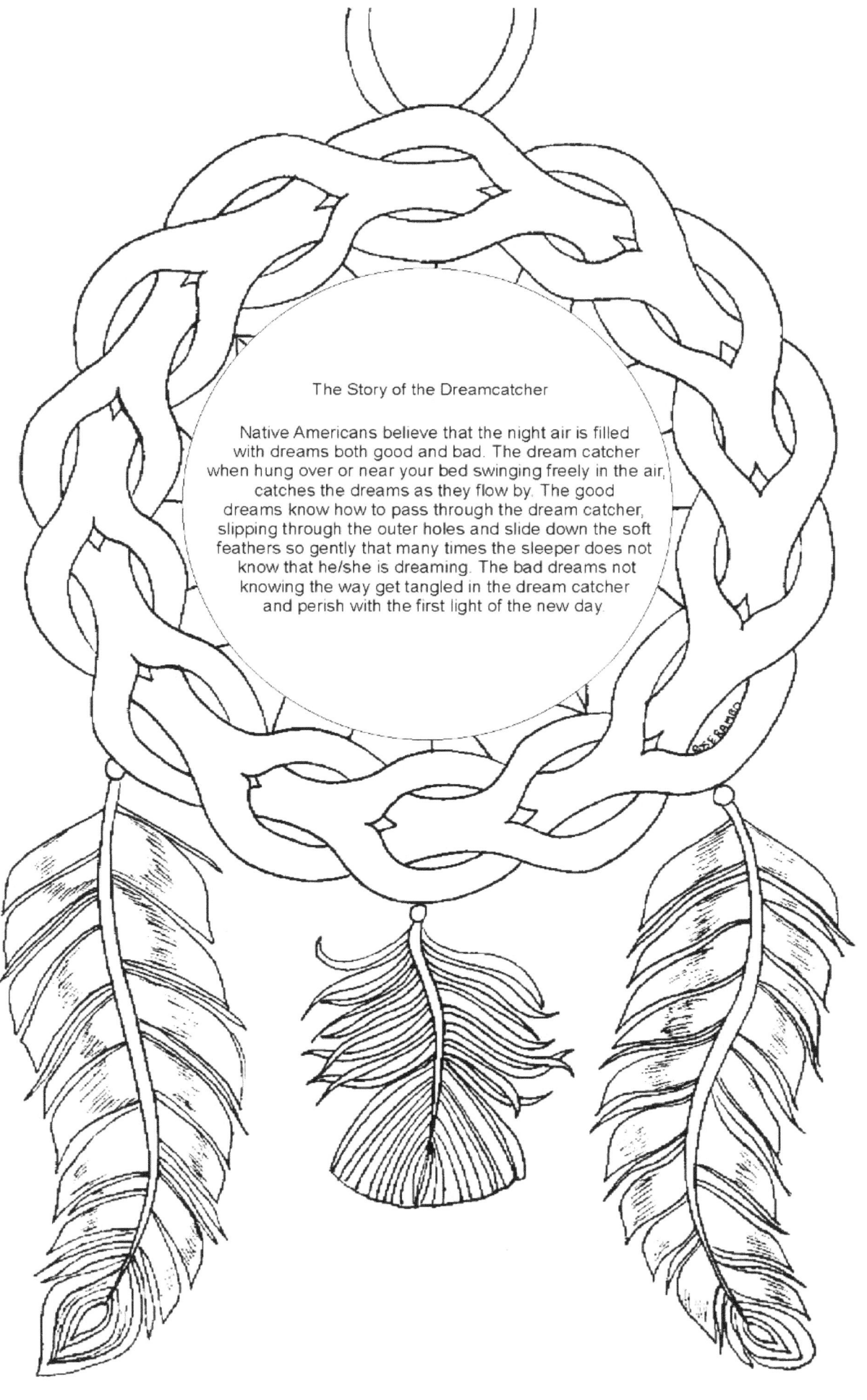

The Story of the Dreamcatcher

Native Americans believe that the night air is filled
with dreams both good and bad. The dream catcher
when hung over or near your bed swinging freely in the air,
catches the dreams as they flow by. The good
dreams know how to pass through the dream catcher,
slipping through the outer holes and slide down the soft
feathers so gently that many times the sleeper does not
know that he/she is dreaming. The bad dreams not
knowing the way get tangled in the dream catcher
and perish with the first light of the new day.

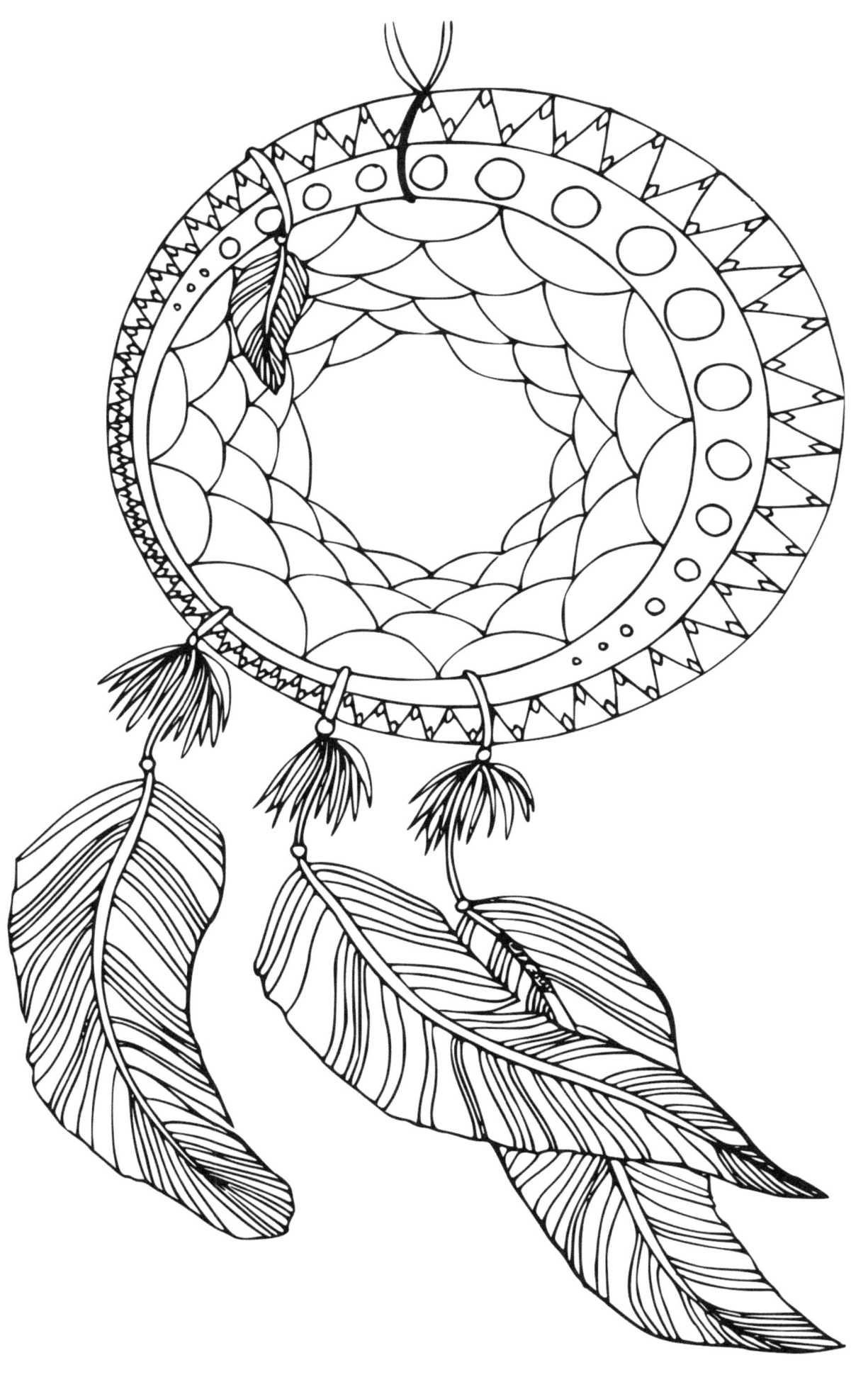

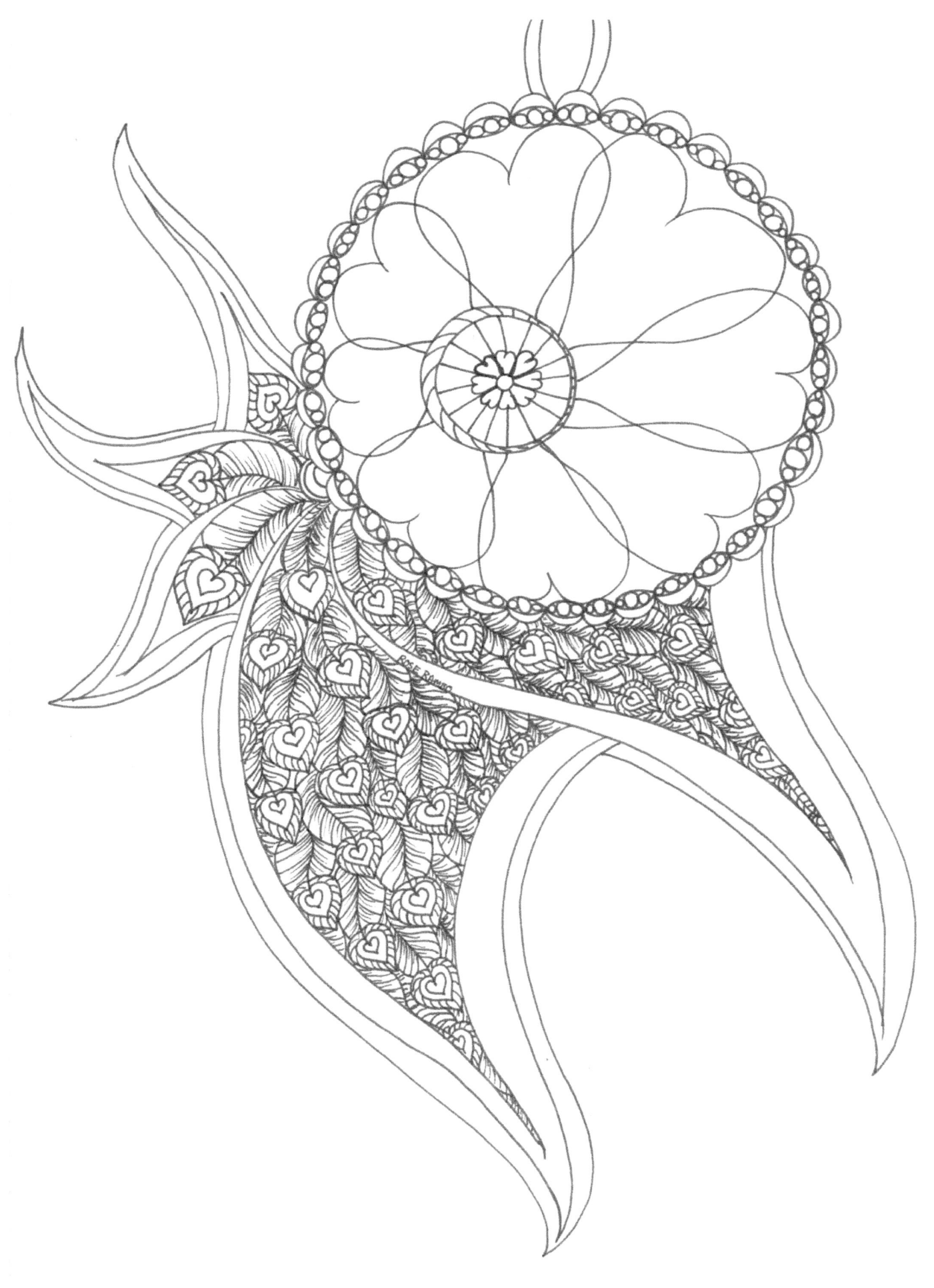

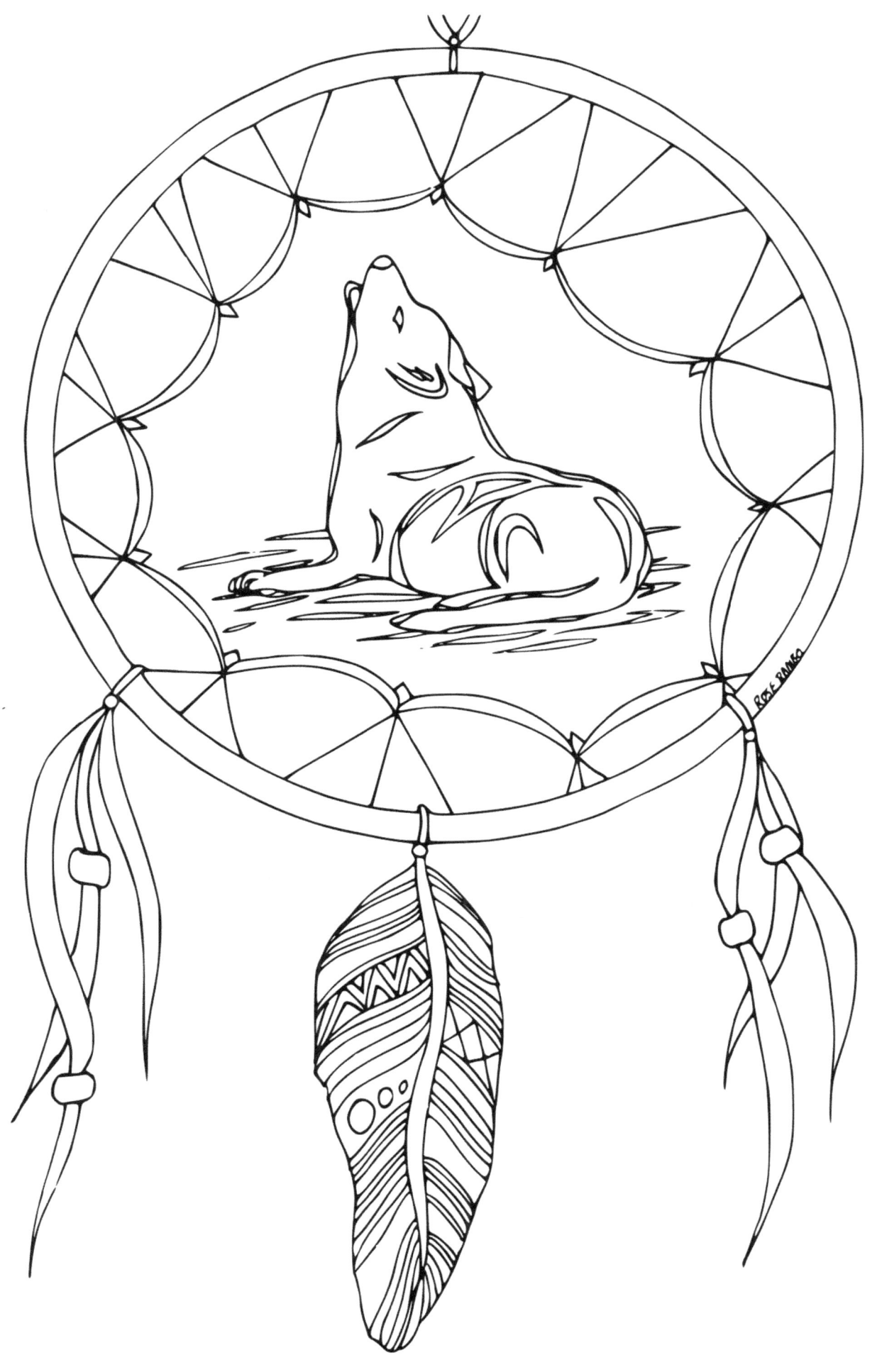

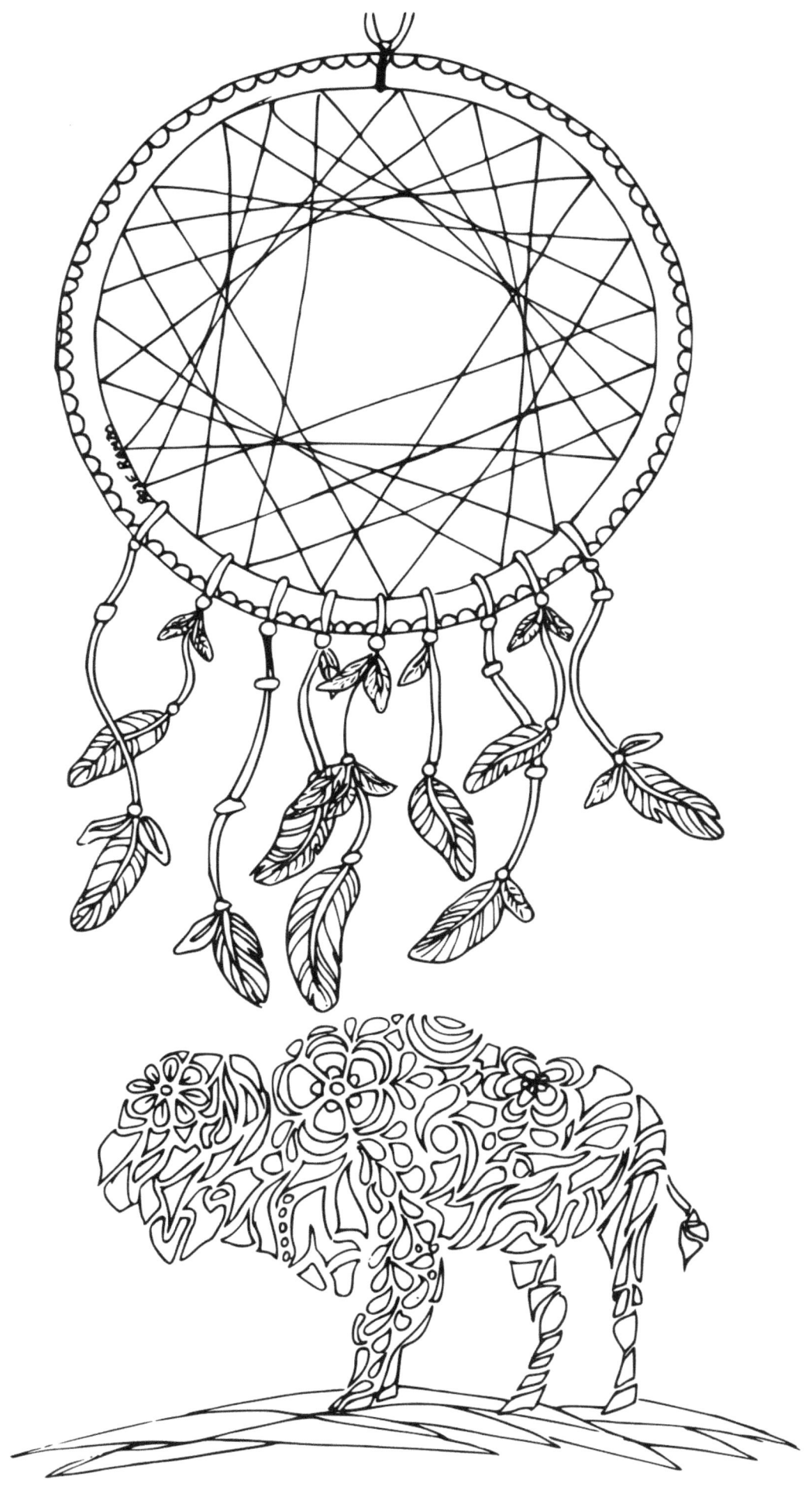

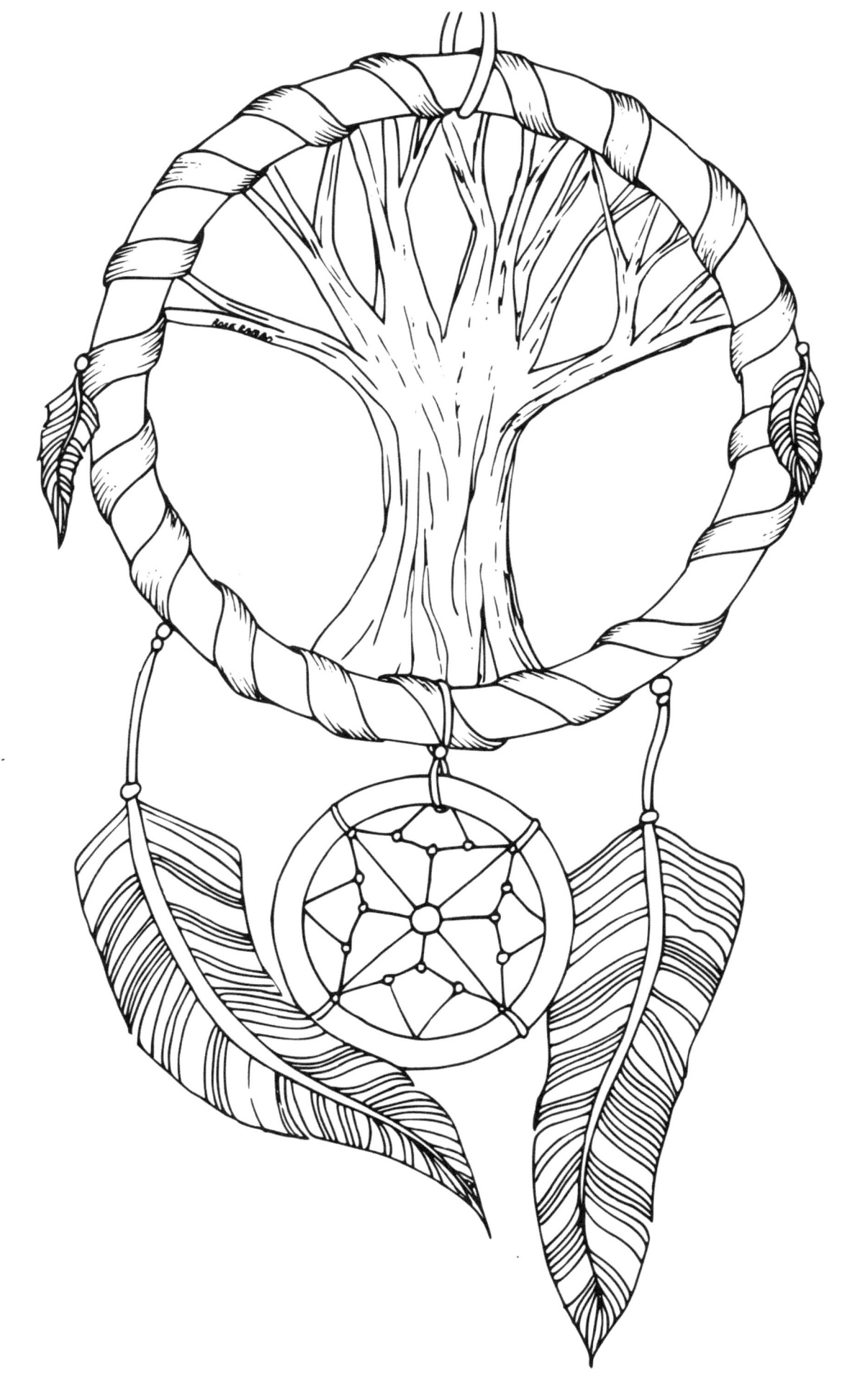

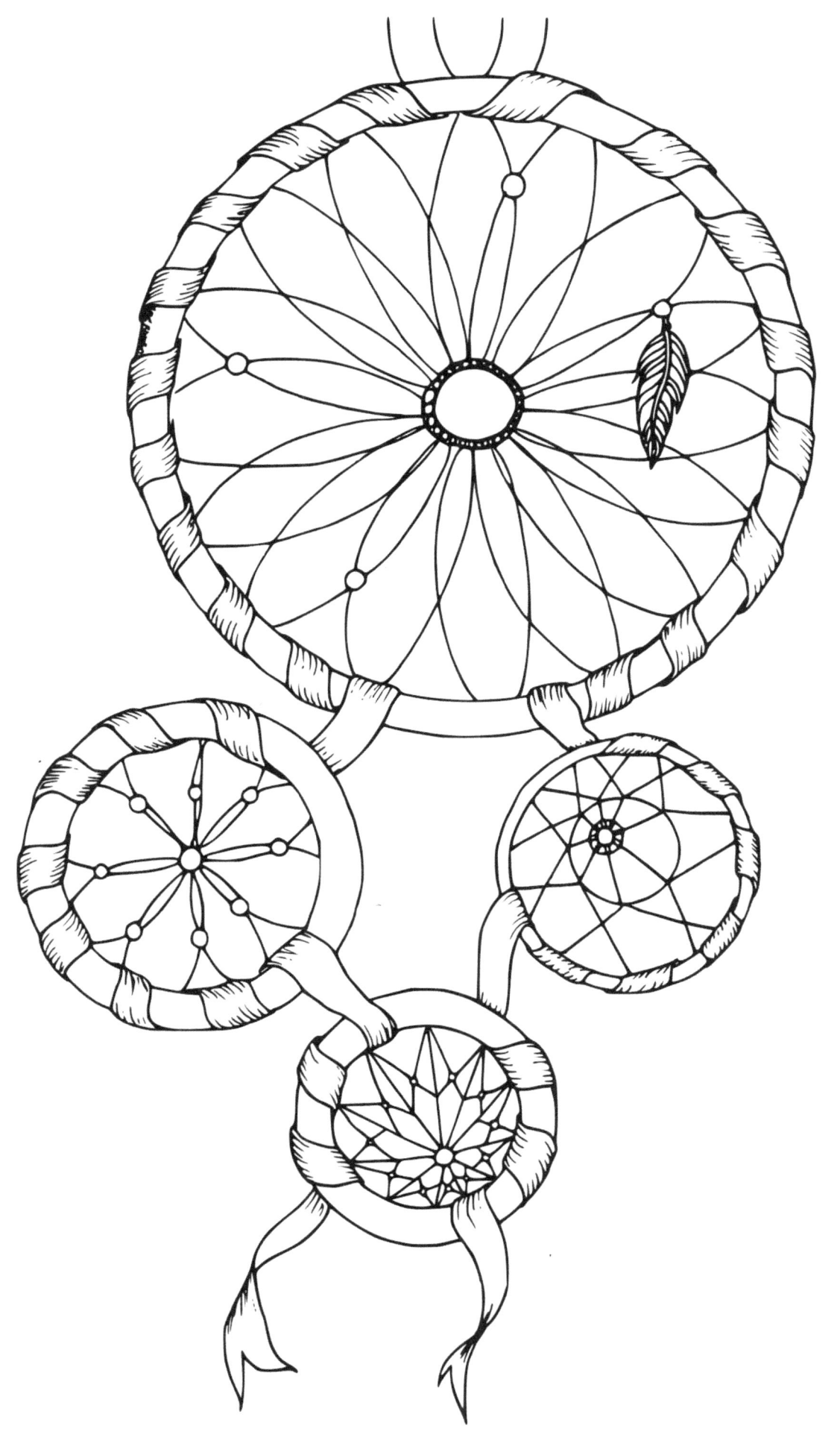

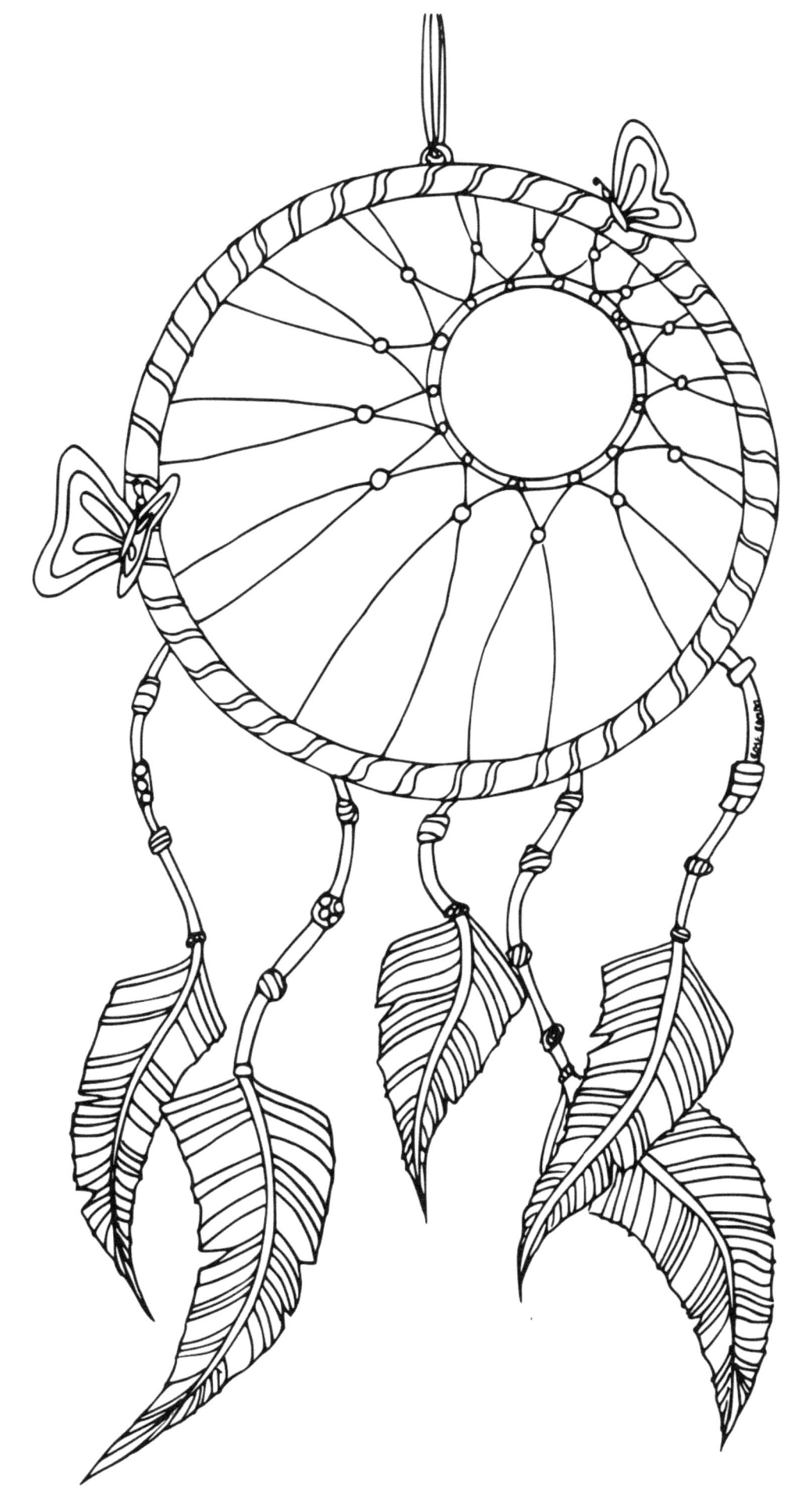

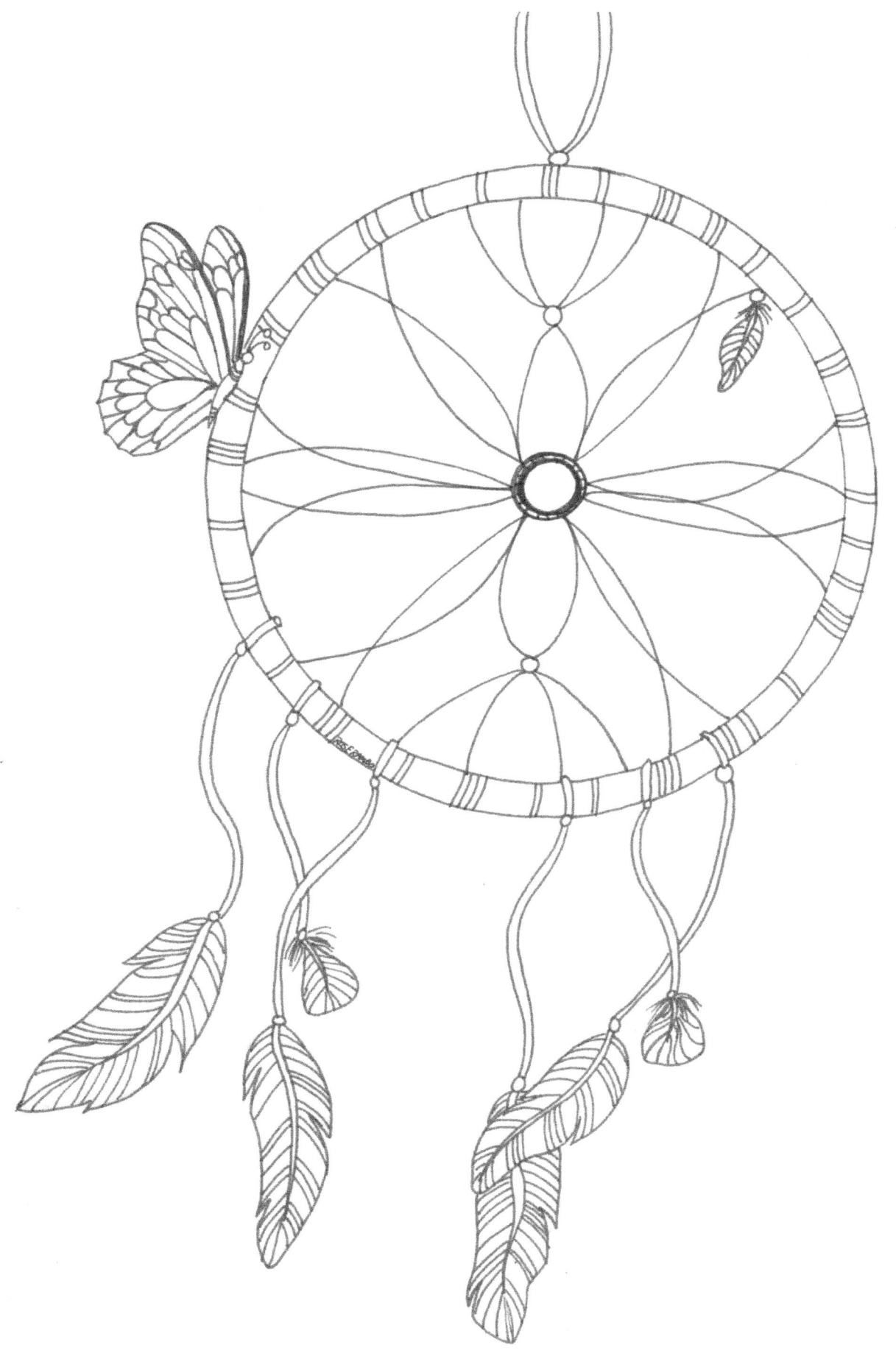

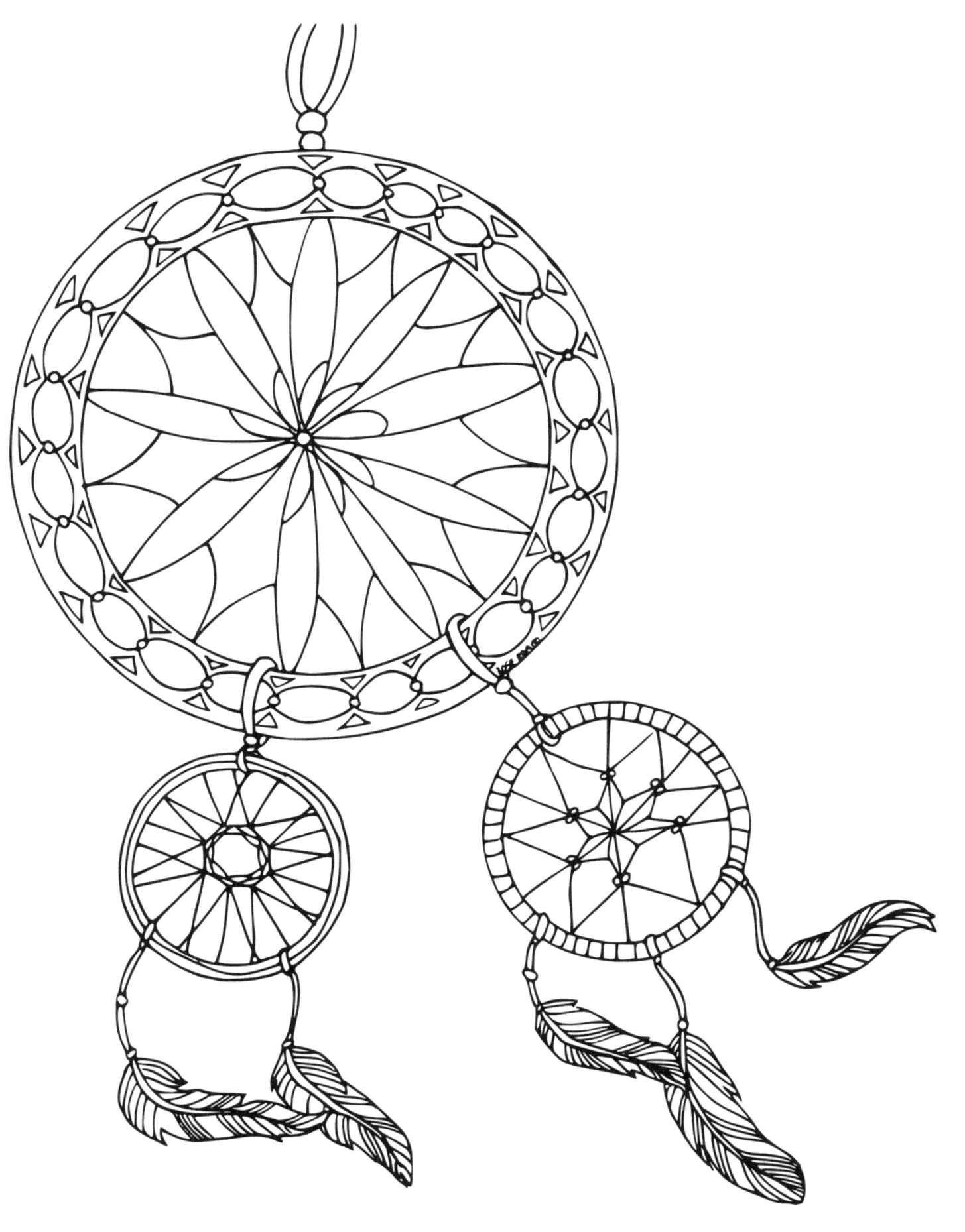

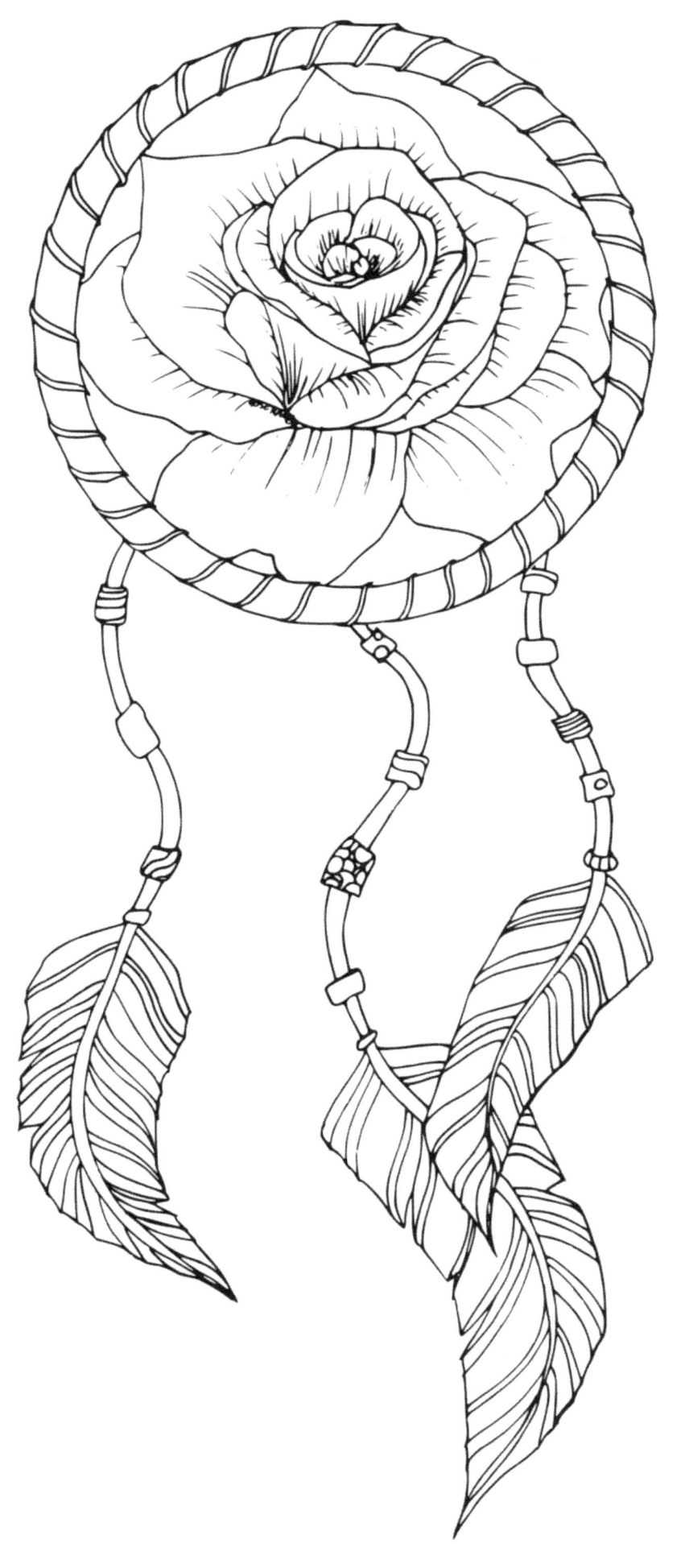

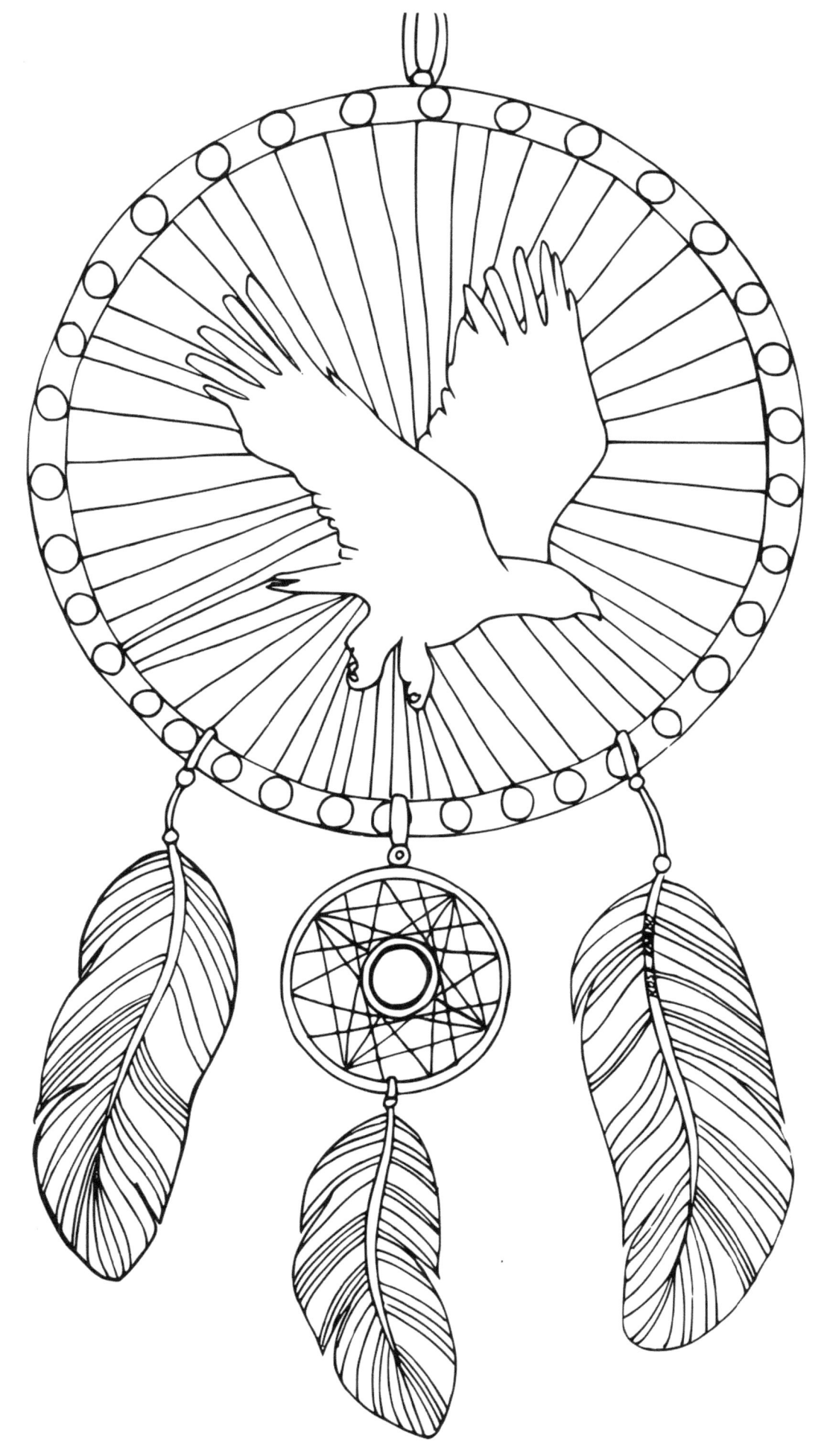

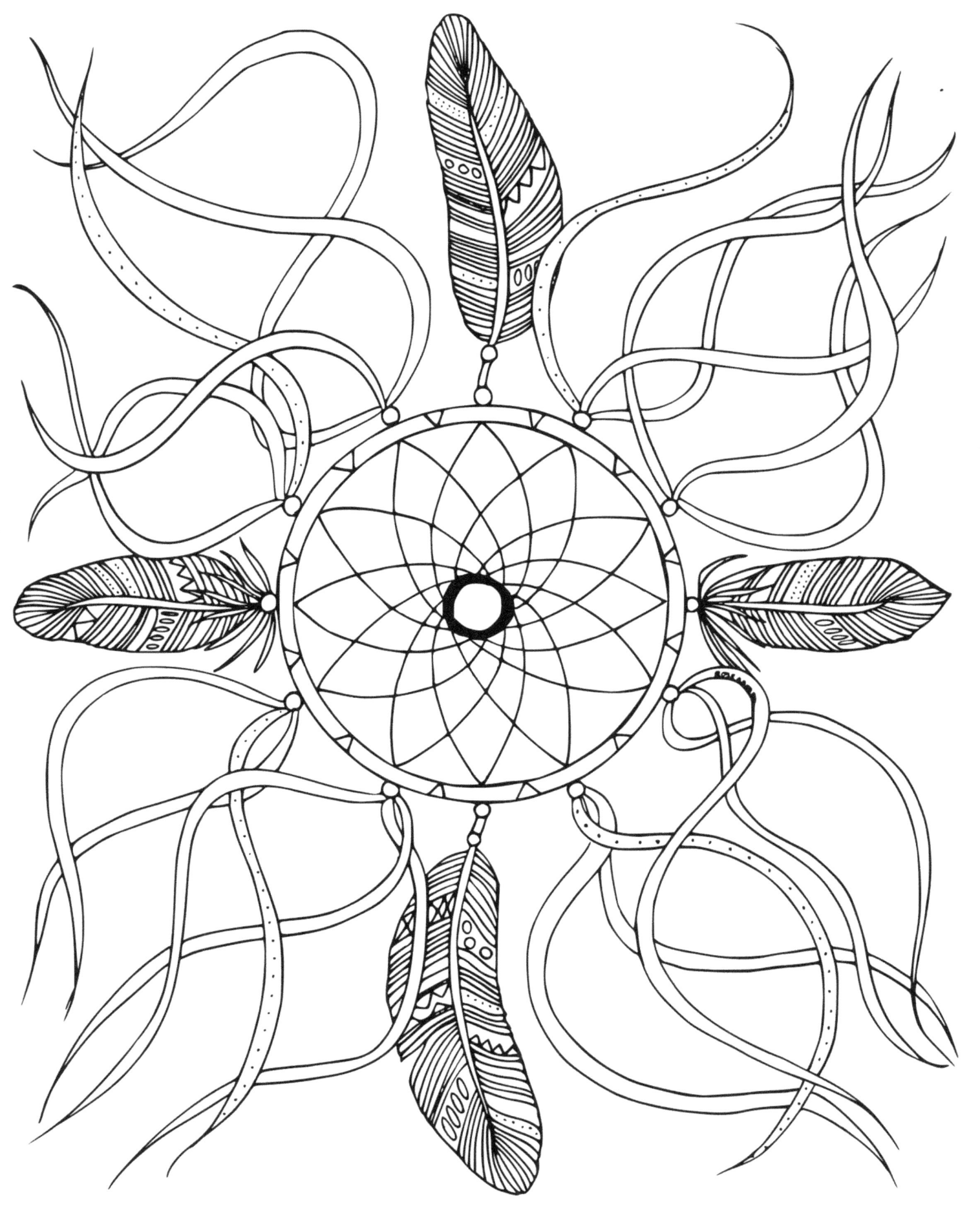

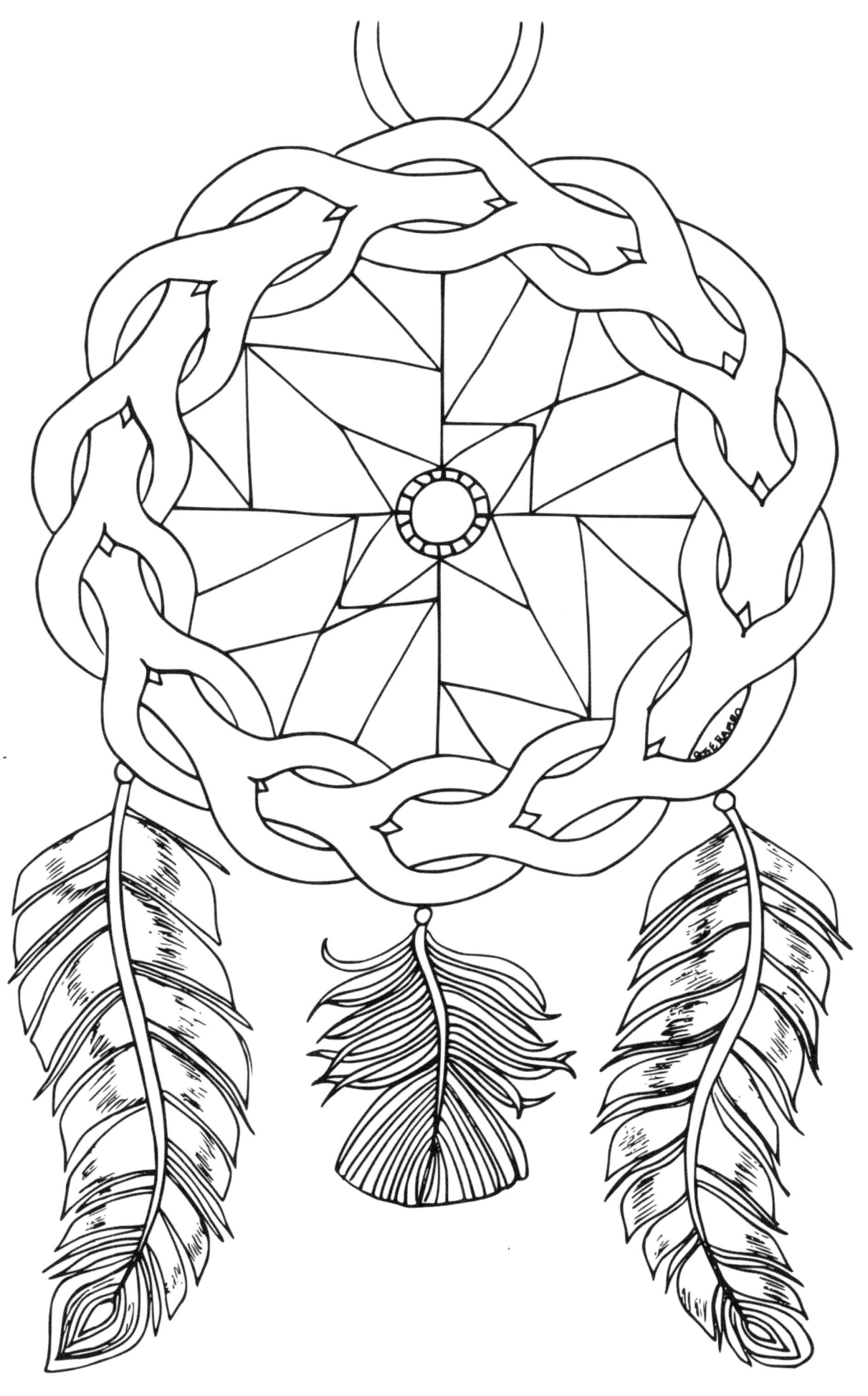

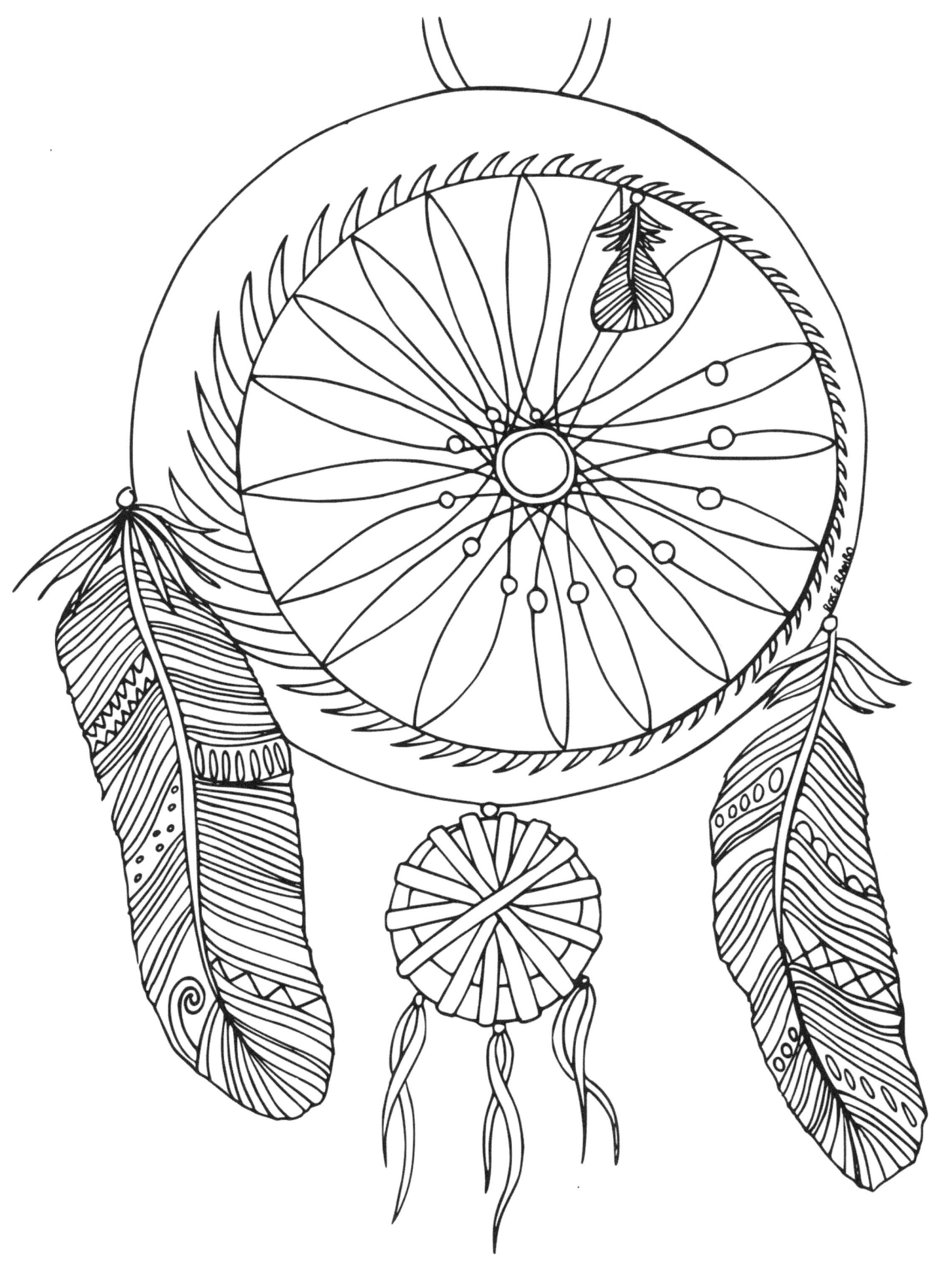

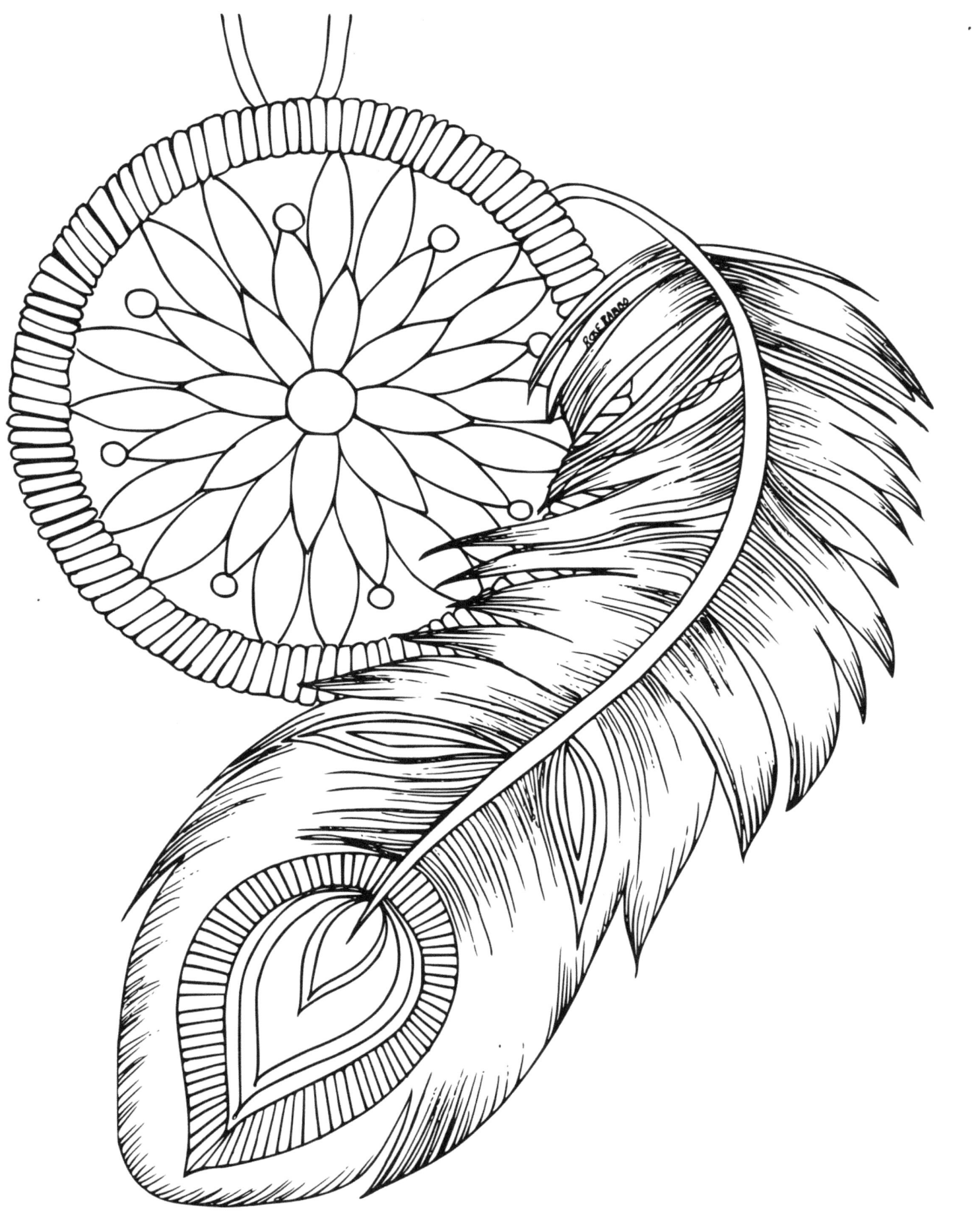

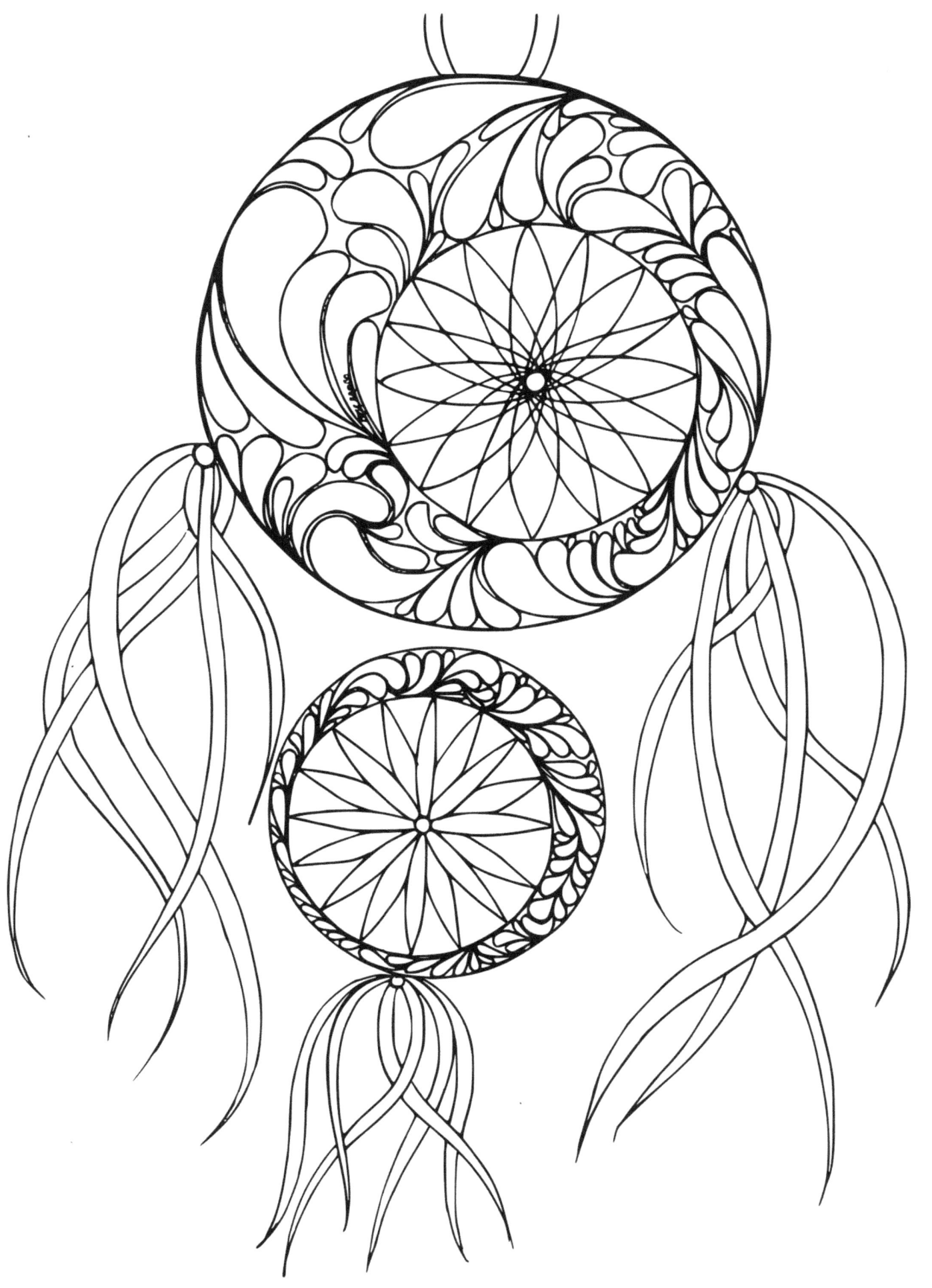

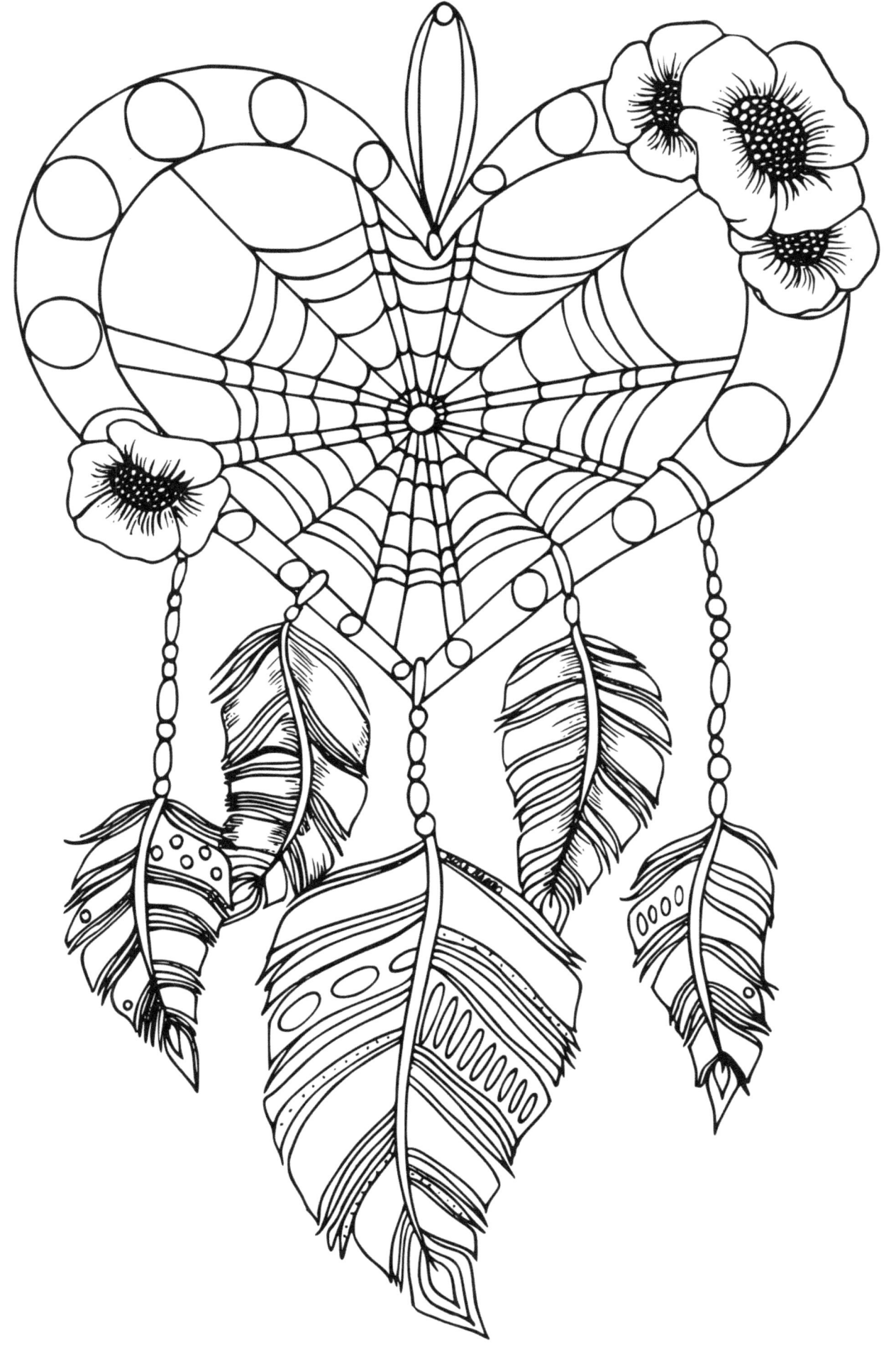

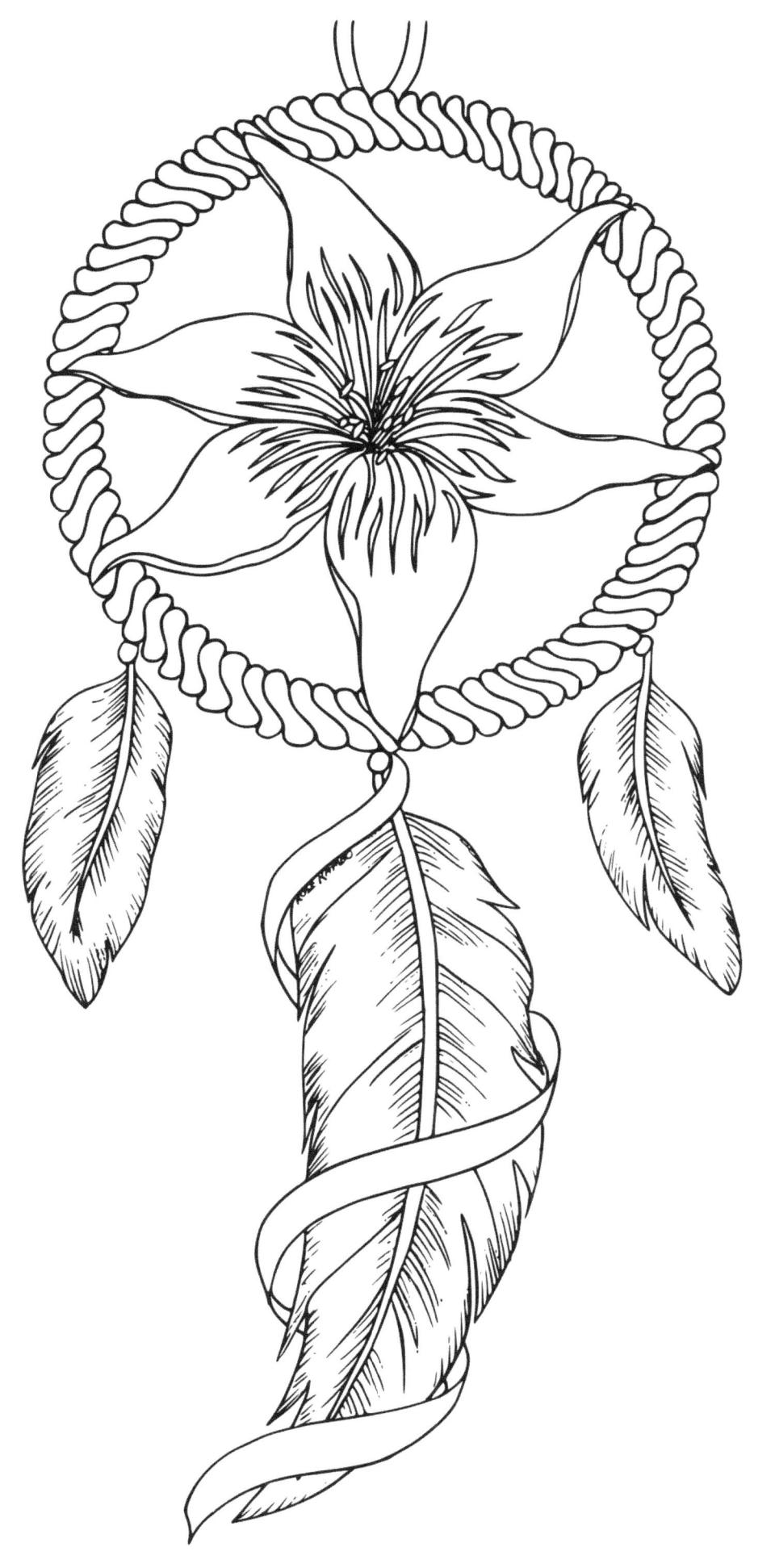

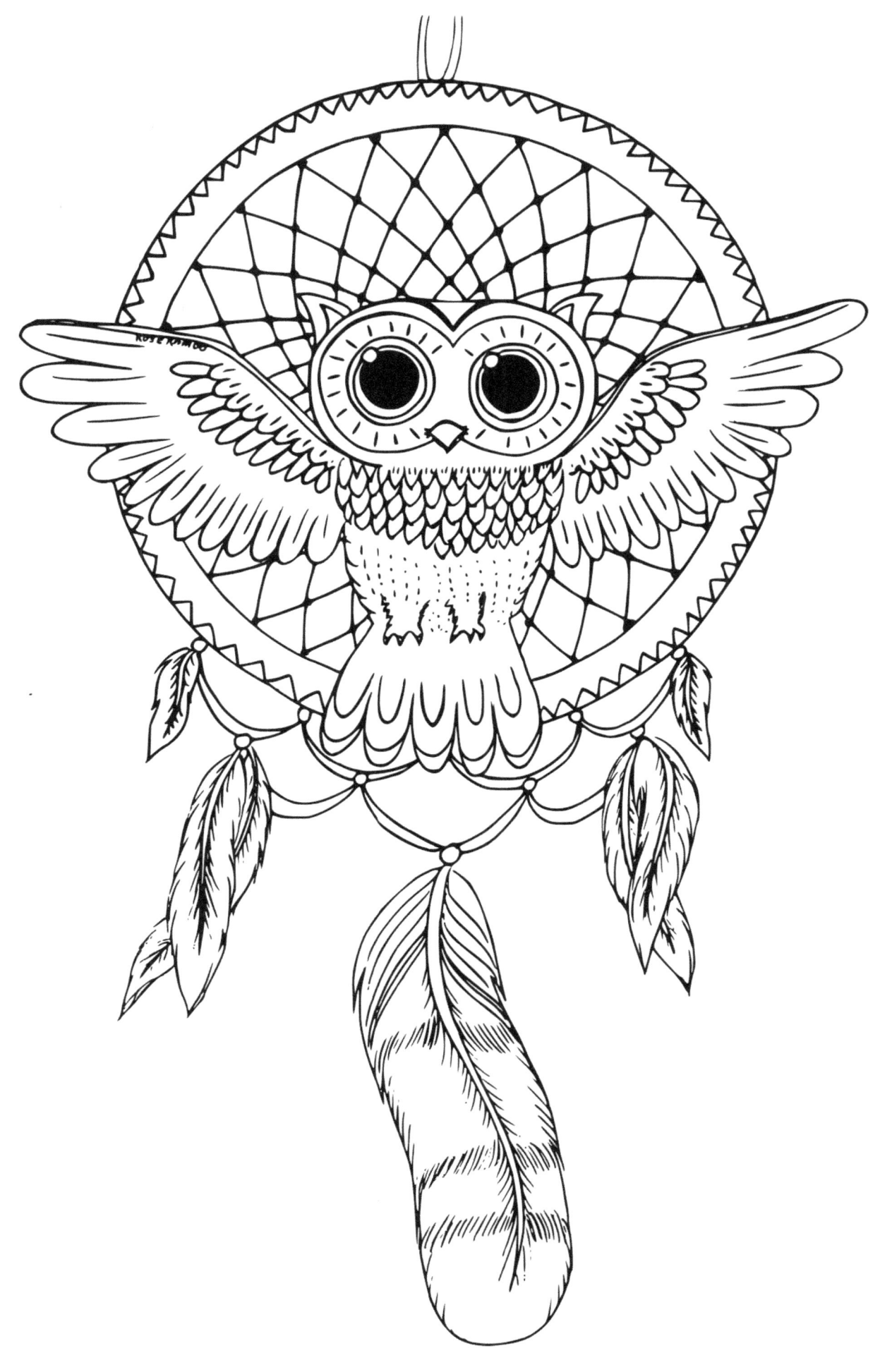

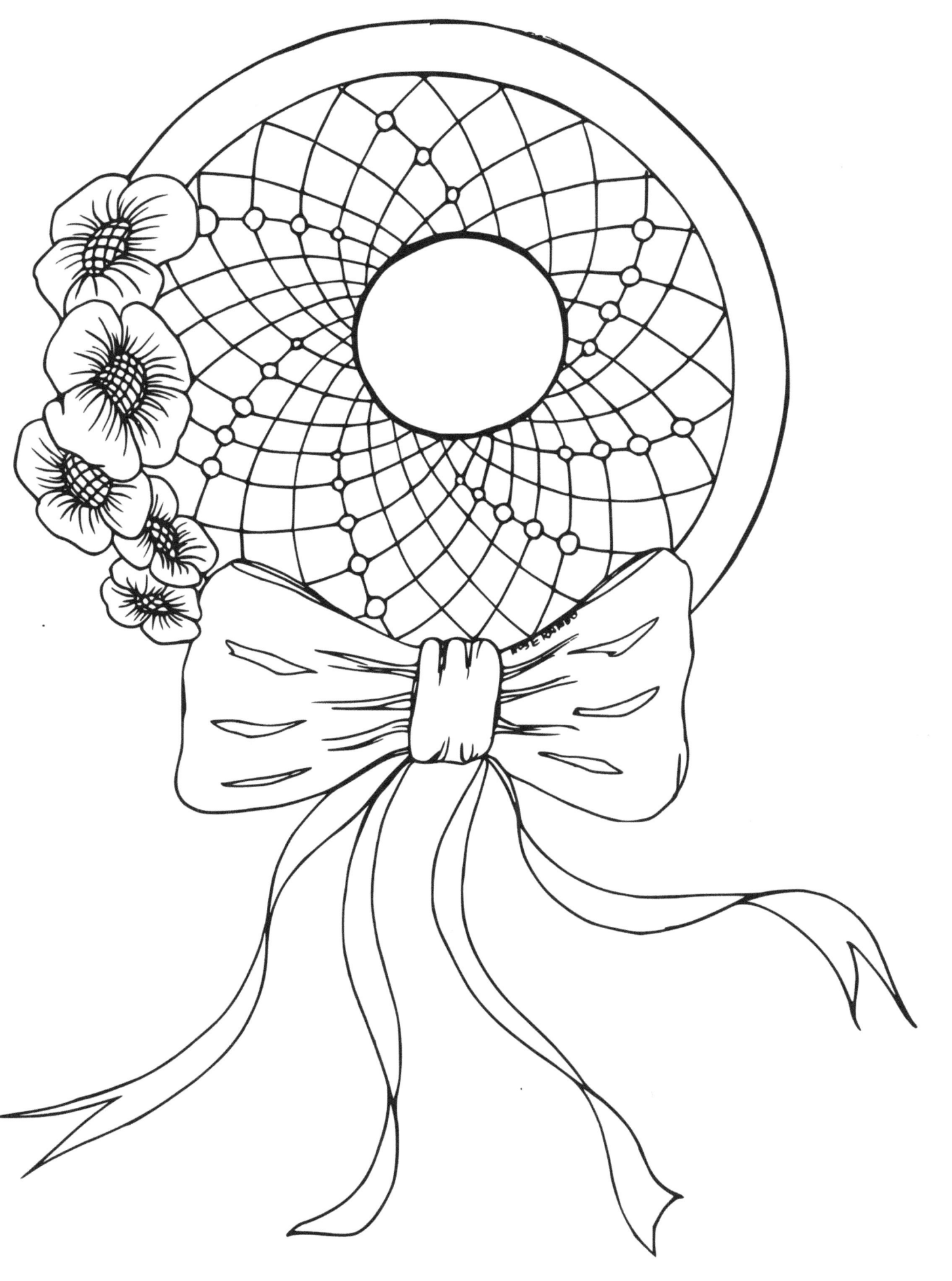

Color Testing Page

Color Testing Page

Rose Rambo is a visionary artist worth following. She has the unique ability to translate the creative inspiration of innocence to paper and canvas. Mrs. Rambo brings joy and inspiration to adults through the creative play of rediscovering the joy of color.

Mrs. Rambo was home schooled and began her studies at Tarrant County College at the age of sixteen. She continued her studies in art at Abilene Christian University. She works in acrylics, watercolor, pen and ink. Rose's attention to detail has created a demand for commissioned portrait work. Her photographic memory provides an endless library of ideas and inspiration.

Rose is a native Texan, born in San Antonio and raised in Fort Worth. She lives with her husband and two cats. Rose looks forward to new opportunities to bring joy, inspiration, and beauty to the world around her.

RoseRambo.com

Etsy.com/shop/vitruvianart

Facebook.com/vitruvianart